MESSI VS

RONALDO

Clash of Legends

FOOTBALL LEGENDS COLLECTION

By

RICHARD DEES

Copyright © 2024, Richard Dees

All rights reserved. No part of this publication may be reproduced, distributed, or transmitted in any form or by any means, including photocopying, recording, or other electronic or mechanical methods, without the prior written permission of the publisher, except in the case of brief quotations embodied in critical reviews and certain other noncommercial uses permitted by copyright law.

ISBN: 9798873348718
Imprint: Independently published

Printed in United Kingdom

First Edition: December, 2023

CONTENTS

Dedication v

CHAPTER 1: Introduction - Setting the Stage 7

CHAPTER 2: Breaking into Professional Football 17

CHAPTER 3: Rise to Prominence 26

CHAPTER 4: Establishing Dominance 43

CHAPTER 5: International Careers 61

CHAPTER 6: Golden Years: Triumphs and Records 69

CHAPTER 7: Iconic Matches and Rivalries 86

CHAPTER 8: Transitions and Adaptations 100

CHAPTER 9: Beyond FOOTBALL 117

CHAPTER 10: Life Off-Pitch 126

CHAPTER 11: Comparison and Contrast 133

CHAPTER 12: Legacy and Continuing Influence 141

CHAPTER 13: Conclusion 147

CHAPTER 14: TRIVIA 151

CHAPTER 15: GUESS WHO 165

Footy Joke Corner 169

Disclaimer 176

DEDICATION

To every young dreamer who has ever kicked a ball,

To the underdogs who rise, and those who stand tall.

To the fans, the families, the teams near and far,

This book is for you, wherever you are.

May you always find joy in the game's simple pleasure, And may your love for football be a treasure forever.

Richard Dees - Lifelong football fan

MESSI VS RONALDO:

CLASH OF LEGENDS

CHAPTER 1: INTRODUCTION - SETTING THE STAGE

""You can overcome anything, if and if only you love something enough." - Lionel Messi

In the world of football, few debates stir as much passion and opinion as the one surrounding Lionel Messi and Cristiano Ronaldo. Considered two of the greatest footballers of all time, their careers have captivated fans and experts alike, sparking discussions in every corner of the globe. This book, "Messi vs Ronaldo:

Clash of Legends," aims to delve deep into this debate, offering a comprehensive comparison of these two football giants.

Our journey begins by setting the stage for this global debate. Across stadiums, social media platforms, and living rooms, the question of who is the superior player often leads to lively, sometimes heated, discussions. This debate transcends borders, age groups, and football affiliations, highlighting the impact these players have had on the sport.

The objective of this book is to present a fair, in-depth comparison of Messi and Ronaldo. We will explore their careers from humble beginnings to becoming global icons, examining their achievements, playing styles, contributions to their teams, and their impact on football. This book is not about declaring a winner but about appreciating the extraordinary qualities of both players.

Our methodology involves a comprehensive examination of their careers. We will look at their early life and beginnings, charting their paths from young, aspiring footballers to professional debutants. We will then explore their rise to prominence, their golden years filled with triumphs and records, and their illustrious international careers.

We will delve into the iconic matches and rivalries that have defined their careers, particularly their face-offs in El Clásico and other key encounters. The book will also explore how Messi and Ronaldo adapted to different teams and leagues, how their playing styles evolved, and how they faced various challenges.

Beyond their on-pitch exploits, we will examine their influence off the pitch, including their impact on global football culture, media portrayal, and involvement in charitable work. Their personal lives, off-pitch endeavours, and the way they have managed their careers outside of football will also be discussed.

In comparing and contrasting Messi and Ronaldo, we will provide a detailed analysis of their playing styles, strengths, weaknesses, and statistical breakdowns of their careers. This will include an examination of their impact on teams, fans, and the history of football.

Finally, we will discuss their legacy and continuing influence, offering insights into how they have shaped the sport and what their roles might be post-retirement. The conclusion will summarize their unparalleled journeys, contributions, and the lasting impact of their rivalry on football.

As we embark on this journey through the careers of Messi and Ronaldo, we invite readers to appreciate the nuances, the moments of brilliance, and the sheer dedication these legends have shown throughout their careers.

"Messi vs Ronaldo: Clash of Legends" is more than just a comparison; it's a celebration of two of the greatest footballers the world has ever seen.

In this book, we turn back the pages to the very start of the journeys of Lionel Messi and Cristiano Ronaldo, exploring their early lives and the initial steps they took in the world of football.

Lionel Messi was born on June 24, 1987, in Rosario, Argentina, into a working-class family. His love for football was evident from a very young age, a passion he shared with his family. Messi joined his first football club, Grandoli, coached by his father, at the tender age of five. His talent was undeniable, as he often played with children much older than him, showcasing skills well beyond his years. Despite his extraordinary talent, Messi faced significant challenges early on. Diagnosed with a growth hormone deficiency at the age of 11, his family struggled to afford his treatment. This challenge, however, would soon lead him to FC Barcelona, where he would start a new chapter in his football career.

Cristiano Ronaldo, born on February 5, 1985, in Funchal, Madeira, Portugal, had a childhood marked by hardship and ambition. Growing up in a modest household, Ronaldo was introduced to football through his father, who worked as a kit man at a local club. His passion for the game was evident from a very young age. Ronaldo played for amateur team Andorinha, where he honed his skills before moving to Nacional, one of Madeira's top teams. At the age of 12, he made a significant move to Sporting CP's academy, marking the start of a journey that would see him become one of football's greats. Ronaldo's early career was not without its challenges. He had to leave his family and adapt to life in Lisbon, facing homesickness and financial difficulties.

Both Messi and Ronaldo showed exceptional talent and dedication from a young age. Their childhoods, although different in environment and circumstances, were united by a deep love for football and a determination to overcome obstacles. These early experiences shaped their character and laid the foundation for their future successes.

Messi's journey from Argentina to Barcelona was a defining moment in his life. Joining La Masia, Barcelona's famed youth academy, he faced the challenge of adapting to a new country and culture at a young age. Despite these obstacles, Messi's talent shone through, and he quickly progressed through the ranks.

Ronaldo's time at Sporting CP was crucial in his development as a footballer. His standout performances for the youth teams brought him recognition as a prodigy. Ronaldo's work ethic, coupled with his natural ability, set him apart from his peers, leading to his debut for Sporting's first team at just 17.

These early chapters in the lives of Messi and Ronaldo highlight the beginnings of their journeys to stardom. From humble origins, facing personal and economic hardships, their paths were marked by resilience, talent, and an unwavering commitment to their dreams.

CHAPTER 2: BREAKING INTO PROFESSIONAL FOOTBALL

"Talent without working hard is nothing" – Cristiano Ronaldo

The journeys of Lionel Messi and Cristiano Ronaldo into the realms of professional football are stories of resilience, talent, and early signs of greatness. This chapter delves into their initial breakthroughs, capturing the moments that marked the beginning of their legendary careers.

Lionel Messi's transition from a young, ambitious player in Argentina to a rising star at Barcelona's famed La Masia academy is a tale of immense talent and determination. Born in Rosario, Argentina, Messi's passion for football was evident from a very young age. His journey took a significant turn when, diagnosed with a growth hormone deficiency, he found an opportunity in Barcelona. At the age of 13, Messi moved to Spain, a move that was as challenging as it was exciting. Adapting to a new country, language, and culture was daunting, but Messi's focus remained unwavering. At La Masia, he was not just another player; he was a prodigy. His ability to control the ball, combined with his vision on the field, set him apart. Messi progressed through the academy ranks with an ease that belied his age, dominating youth tournaments and drawing attention from the senior team's coaching staff.

Cristiano Ronaldo's path to professional football had its own unique trajectory. Born in Funchal, Madeira, Portugal, Ronaldo's journey began at local clubs Andorinha and Nacional. His talent was undeniable, and it wasn't long before he caught the attention of Sporting CP, one of Portugal's top football academies. At just 12 years old, Ronaldo left Madeira for Lisbon, a move that was both an emotional and physical challenge. At Sporting CP, Ronaldo's skills flourished. His speed, agility, and flair on the ball made him stand out among his peers. His work ethic was unparalleled, often spending hours training beyond the scheduled sessions. Ronaldo's rise through Sporting's ranks was meteoric, and by the age of 16, he was already catching the eye of Europe's top clubs.

For both Messi and Ronaldo, these early years in professional football were formative. They were not only developing their skills but also learning to adapt to new environments and expectations. The pressure of playing for renowned clubs could have been overwhelming, but Messi and Ronaldo thrived under it, showing early signs of the mental strength and resilience that would define their careers.

As Lionel Messi and Cristiano Ronaldo progressed through the ranks of their respective clubs, their talent and potential began to manifest in significant ways, marking the start of their ascent in professional football.

Lionel Messi's early days at FC Barcelona were a blend of hard work, adaptation, and sheer brilliance. At La Masia, Barcelona's youth academy, Messi's skills were refined under the tutelage of some of the best youth coaches. His playing style, characterized by incredible close control, agility, and an innate understanding of the game, fit seamlessly with Barcelona's philosophy. Messi's progression through the academy ranks was rapid, and his performances in youth tournaments were nothing short of exceptional. He quickly caught the eye of the first-team coaches and was soon training with the senior squad. Messi's first-team debut for Barcelona came on November 16, 2003, in a friendly match against Porto, making him the youngest player to ever play for Barcelona at that time. This debut was more than just a milestone; it was the beginning of an era.

Cristiano Ronaldo's journey at Sporting CP culminated in a life-changing moment that would catapult his career to new heights. Ronaldo's performances for Sporting's youth teams had already made him a player to watch. His debut for Sporting's senior team came on October 7, 2002, against Moreirense, where he scored two goals, announcing his arrival on the professional stage. However, it was a pre-season friendly match against Manchester United in August 2003 that changed the course of his career. Ronaldo's dazzling performance against United's seasoned defenders caught the attention of Sir Alex Ferguson, Manchester United's manager. Impressed by his skill, speed, and potential, Ferguson decided to sign Ronaldo, marking the start of a new chapter in the young Portuguese player's career.

At Manchester United, Ronaldo was thrust into one of the world's most competitive football leagues. His first season at United was a period of learning and adaptation. Ronaldo's style, characterized by flashy dribbling and incredible athleticism, was initially met with mixed reactions. However, his determination to improve was evident. Under the mentorship of Sir Alex Ferguson and surrounded by experienced teammates, Ronaldo's game began to evolve. He developed into a more complete player, honing his goal-scoring ability and tactical understanding of the game. His first goal for Manchester United came on November 1,

2003, against Portsmouth, a stunning free-kick that gave fans a glimpse of what was to come.

For both Messi and Ronaldo, these early years in their professional careers were crucial. They were not only adapting to the rigors of professional football but also making their mark. Their talent, work ethic, and resilience during this period laid the foundation for what would become legendary careers. They faced challenges and expectations with a maturity beyond their years, continuously pushing themselves to excel and proving that they were destined for greatness.

CHAPTER 3: RISE TO PROMINENCE

""You have to fight to achieve your dreams. You have to sacrifice and work hard for it." - Lionel Messi

The journey of Lionel Messi and Cristiano Ronaldo into the world of top-tier football is a testament to their extraordinary talent and unwavering determination. This chapter focuses on their rise to prominence, exploring how they broke into the first teams of Barcelona and Manchester United, respectively, and began to make their mark in professional football.

Lionel Messi's integration into Barcelona's first team was a gradual process, marked by significant milestones that showcased his growing importance to the team. Under the management of Frank Rijkaard, Messi began to get more playing time, and with each opportunity, he demonstrated why he was touted as a future star. His La Liga debut came on October 16, 2004, against Espanyol, making him the youngest player to ever play in the league for Barcelona at that time. But it was in the 2004-2005 season where Messi truly announced himself. On May 1, 2005, in a match against Albacete, Messi scored his first goal for Barcelona's senior team, a delicate lob assisted by Ronaldinho. This goal not only marked his first official goal for the team but also signified the passing of the torch from Ronaldinho, then Barcelona's star player, to Messi.

Cristiano Ronaldo's rise to prominence at Manchester United was a journey marked by rapid development and adaptation. After his transfer from Sporting CP, Ronaldo was immediately thrust into the spotlight of the Premier League. His debut for Manchester United came on August 16, 2003, against Bolton Wanderers, where his performance off the bench was a dazzling display of skill and speed, earning him a standing ovation from the fans. Ronaldo's first season at United was about adaptation. He worked tirelessly to refine his skills, focusing on his end product and decision-making. His first goal for Manchester United, a free-kick against Portsmouth on November 1, 2003, showcased his potential and hinted at the impact he would have in English football.

For both Messi and Ronaldo, their early years in top-tier football were characterized by rapid growth and increasing recognition. Messi, with his exceptional dribbling ability, vision, and natural goal-scoring instinct, was quickly becoming an integral part of Barcelona's attack. His partnership with Ronaldinho and Samuel Eto'o was crucial, as he learned from their experience and skill.

Ronaldo, on the other hand, was making a name for himself in the Premier League with his unique style of play. His speed, flair, and ability to take on defenders made him a fan favorite at Manchester United. Under the guidance of Sir Alex Ferguson, Ronaldo was developing into a more complete and effective player, blending his natural talent with a newfound tactical understanding of the game.

As Lionel Messi and Cristiano Ronaldo solidified their positions in their respective teams, their influence on the pitch began to grow exponentially, marked by key performances and individual accolades that highlighted their burgeoning status as world-class talents.

Lionel Messi's growth at Barcelona continued to be meteoric. The 2005-2006 season was particularly significant, as Messi began to establish himself not just as a talented young player, but as a crucial member of the first team. His performances in the league and in Europe were increasingly influential. A standout moment came in March 2007 during a match against Real Madrid. Messi scored a hat-trick, becoming the first player since Ivan Zamorano (for Real Madrid in the 1994-1995 season) to do so in El Clásico. This performance wasn't just a display of his extraordinary talent; it was a statement that Messi was ready to be Barcelona's leading figure.

Cristiano Ronaldo's rise at Manchester United was equally impressive. The 2006-2007 season marked a turning point in his career. Ronaldo had begun to transform into a goal-scoring winger, blending his natural flair with a more effective and efficient playing style. His performances helped propel Manchester United to a Premier League title, their first in four years. Ronaldo's contributions were recognized as he won his first PFA Players' Player of the Year and the FWA Footballer of the Year awards. These accolades were a testament to his growing influence in English football and his evolution into one of the game's premier players.

Both Messi and Ronaldo were now not just promising talents; they were key players for their teams, capable of changing the course of games with their skills. Their ability to deliver in crucial matches and their consistency in performance began to draw comparisons and sparked debates among fans and pundits about their standing in the world of football.

Messi's playing style, characterized by his low center of gravity, incredible balance, and close ball control, coupled with his vision and playmaking ability, made him a formidable force on the field. He was not just a goal scorer; he was a creator, a player who could dictate the flow of the game.

Ronaldo, with his athleticism, skill, and goal-scoring ability, had become a symbol of modern football. His versatility allowed him to play across the front line, making him a constant threat to defenses. His work ethic and desire to continuously improve were evident in his performances, as he began to add more goals and assists to his game.

The ascension of Lionel Messi and Cristiano Ronaldo in the world of football continued to gain momentum, as both players started to etch their names in the annals of the sport through remarkable performances and significant contributions to their teams.

Lionel Messi's role in Barcelona's successes became increasingly pivotal. In the 2006-2007 season, Messi continued to showcase his exceptional talent, contributing crucial goals and assists. His ability to change the game with his individual skill was evident, but it was his understanding of Barcelona's playing style and his synergy with teammates that truly set him apart. Messi's performance against Getafe in the Copa del Rey, where he scored a goal reminiscent of Diego Maradona's famous 'Goal of the Century', was a clear indication of his growing stature in the football world.

Cristiano Ronaldo's transformation into one of the world's best was becoming more apparent with each passing season. The 2007-2008 season was a standout year for Ronaldo at Manchester United. He was the driving force behind United's successful campaign, which saw them win both the Premier League and the UEFA Champions League. Ronaldo's 42 goals in all competitions were crucial to these triumphs. His ability to score from various positions, whether it be through blistering long-range efforts, free-kicks, or headers, showcased his versatility and lethal goal-scoring ability. Ronaldo's performance in the Champions League final, where he scored the opening goal, underscored his importance to the team.

By now, Messi and Ronaldo were not just rising stars; they were established world-class players, consistently delivering performances that influenced the outcomes of matches and tournaments. Their individual accolades started to pile up, with Messi being recognized as the FIFA World Player of the Year in 2009 and Ronaldo receiving the same honor in 2008.

Their styles, while distinct, were equally effective. Messi, with his mesmerizing dribbling ability, incredible vision, and natural goal-scoring instinct, was a player who could create and score with equal proficiency. His low center of gravity and quick feet allowed him to navigate through tight spaces with ease, making him a constant threat to any defense.

Ronaldo, known for his physical prowess, speed, and aerial ability, was a player who could change the game in an instant. His dedication to improving his physique and skills made him one of the most complete forwards in the game. Ronaldo's ability to perform in crucial moments, especially in big matches, was a testament to his mental strength and competitive nature.

As Lionel Messi and Cristiano Ronaldo continued to excel in their respective leagues, their rivalry began to take a central stage in the world of football, captivating fans and experts alike with their extraordinary performances and contrasting styles.

The rivalry between Messi and Ronaldo, particularly evident during Ronaldo's time at Real Madrid, added an extra layer of excitement to La Liga and the UEFA Champions League. Their head-to-head battles, especially in El Clásico matches between Barcelona and Real Madrid, were highly anticipated events that drew global attention. Each El Clásico became not just a contest between two of the world's most renowned clubs, but also a showcase of the talents of Messi and Ronaldo. These matches were often decisive in the title race in La Liga and were marked by memorable performances from both players.

In European competitions, particularly the UEFA Champions League, Messi and Ronaldo continued to set records and amass accolades. Messi's ability to perform on the biggest stage was evident in Barcelona's Champions League triumphs in 2009 and 2011, where he played pivotal roles, including scoring in both finals. His performances helped solidify Barcelona's status as one of the best teams in Europe.

Ronaldo, on the other hand, became synonymous with the Champions League, particularly noted for his goal-scoring exploits. His performances in the knockout stages of the competition were often decisive, helping Real Madrid to secure consecutive Champions League titles, including an unprecedented three in a row from 2016 to 2018. Ronaldo's remarkable ability to score in crucial matches solidified his reputation as one of the greatest players in the history of the competition.

Their impact extended beyond their clubs and individual accolades. Messi and Ronaldo became the faces of modern football, influencing the global narrative around the sport. Their rivalry was not just about who scored more goals or won more awards; it was about two contrasting football philosophies and styles. Messi, often described as a naturally gifted player with extraordinary dribbling and playmaking abilities, contrasted with Ronaldo, known for his physical prowess, work ethic, and incredible goal-scoring ability.

This period in their careers was not just about their individual achievements but also about how they pushed each other to greater heights. Their rivalry brought the best out of each other, and their consistent performances raised the standards of what was considered possible in football.

CHAPTER 4: ESTABLISHING DOMINANCE

"I don't want to be like anyone. I want to be myself." – Cristiano Ronaldo

The era of Lionel Messi and Cristiano Ronaldo in the late 2000s and early 2010s was marked by their unparalleled dominance in world football. This part of the chapter focuses on how they not only continued to excel individually but also how they elevated their teams to new heights.

Lionel Messi's influence at Barcelona went beyond his individual brilliance. His synergy with teammates, especially noted in his partnership with Xavi Hernandez and Andres Iniesta, was integral to Barcelona's success. This period saw Barcelona dominate both Spanish and European football, with Messi as the focal point of their attack. His ability to combine individual skill with team play made Barcelona one of the most feared teams in the world. Under the management of Pep Guardiola, Messi thrived, adapting to different tactical formations and roles. His flexibility and understanding of the game were key in Barcelona's treble-winning season in 2008-2009, where they won La Liga, the Copa del Rey, and the UEFA Champions League. Messi's role in this success was pivotal, as he topped the scoring charts and provided numerous assists.

Cristiano Ronaldo's time at Real Madrid saw him become not just a star player but a leader on and off the pitch. His work ethic, determination, and constant drive for improvement were infectious, setting high standards for the entire team. Ronaldo played a crucial role in Real Madrid's successes, particularly in their UEFA Champions League triumphs. His ability to perform in crucial matches, combined with his leadership qualities, were instrumental in Real Madrid winning four Champions League titles during his time at the club, including three consecutively from 2016 to 2018. Ronaldo's impact was not limited to goal-scoring; he also evolved into a more complete player, contributing significantly in terms of assists and overall play.

The dominance of Messi and Ronaldo during this period was not just about their performances on the pitch. It was about how they became leaders and role models for their teammates. Their commitment to excellence, dedication to the sport, and ability to consistently perform at the highest level set a benchmark for others. They were not just players; they were symbols of ambition and excellence.

Messi's connection with his Barcelona teammates was evident in the seamless way they played. The understanding and on-field chemistry he shared with his colleagues were a significant factor in Barcelona's attractive and effective style of play. Messi's humility and team-oriented approach, despite his superstar status, endeared him to his teammates and fans alike.

Ronaldo, known for his competitiveness and winning mentality, brought a level of professionalism and dedication to Real Madrid that elevated the team's overall performance. His influence extended beyond the field, as he often took on a mentoring role for younger players, sharing his experience and knowledge.

Chapter 4: Establishing Dominance - Part 2

During this era, both Lionel Messi and Cristiano Ronaldo amassed a staggering array of individual achievements, setting new records and consistently pushing the boundaries of what was thought possible in football.

Lionel Messi's list of personal accolades in this period is extensive. He won the Ballon d'Or multiple times, solidifying his place among the greatest players of all time. Messi's ability to consistently produce moments of magic, coupled with his impressive goal-scoring and assist records, made him a perennial favorite for the award. His performance in the 2011-2012 season was particularly remarkable, as he set a new record for the most goals scored in a single European club season. Messi's influence extended beyond statistics; his style of play, characterized by mesmerizing dribbling, incredible vision, and sublime finishing, redefined expectations of what a forward could achieve.

Cristiano Ronaldo's time at Real Madrid was equally marked by individual brilliance. He, too, won the Ballon d'Or multiple times, a testament to his status as one of the world's best players. Ronaldo's goal-scoring feats were extraordinary, breaking numerous records, including becoming Real Madrid's all-time top goal scorer in just six seasons. His performances in the Champions

League were particularly notable, where he consistently ranked as one of the tournament's top scorers. Ronaldo's physicality, speed, and lethal finishing ability made him a formidable opponent for any defense.

The rivalry between Messi and Ronaldo was not just a matter of fan and media speculation; it was reflected in their pursuit of excellence. Each pushed the other to perform better, setting new standards in football. Their rivalry was a driving force in their careers, as they competed not just for titles and awards, but also for the unofficial title of the world's best player.

Beyond their on-pitch exploits, Messi and Ronaldo became influential figures in football culture. Their styles, personalities, and performances influenced a generation of young players and fans. They became icons of the sport, representing two different philosophies and styles of play. Messi, often portrayed as the natural, gifted talent, contrasted with Ronaldo, seen as the epitome of hard work and dedication.

Their dominance during this period was not just about the goals they scored or the matches they won; it was about how they elevated the sport itself. They brought excitement, creativity, and an unparalleled level of skill to football, captivating audiences worldwide.

Lionel Messi and Cristiano Ronaldo's influence extended beyond their club careers, as they both played pivotal roles for their national teams. Their participation in international tournaments added another dimension to their careers, providing them with opportunities to showcase their talents on an even larger stage.

Lionel Messi's journey with the Argentina national team has been one of highs and lows. Despite his phenomenal success at Barcelona, international glory initially eluded him. Messi was a key player for Argentina in several Copa America tournaments and FIFA World Cup campaigns. His performances in these tournaments were often outstanding, but the team fell short of winning titles, leading to criticism in some quarters. However, Messi's commitment to the national team never wavered. His leadership and influence were evident, as he often carried the team with his performances. Notably, Messi led Argentina to the finals of the 2014 FIFA World Cup and the Copa America in 2015 and 2016, though they finished as runners-up in all three tournaments.

Cristiano Ronaldo's impact on the Portugal national team has been significant. His leadership and goal-scoring ability have been vital to Portugal's successes. One of Ronaldo's most notable achievements came in the 2016 UEFA European Championship. Ronaldo's performances throughout the tournament were crucial, leading Portugal to the final. Although he was injured early in the final match against France, his encouragement and support from the sidelines were pivotal as Portugal went on to win the tournament, giving Ronaldo his first major international trophy.

Both Messi and Ronaldo's contributions to their national teams highlighted different aspects of their personalities and playing styles. Messi, often seen as a more reserved figure, let his football do the talking. His ability to create opportunities and score crucial goals made him an indispensable part of the Argentina team. Ronaldo, with his charismatic and determined personality, often inspired his teammates through both his performances and leadership.

Their roles in international football further cemented their places as not just great club players but also as global football icons. Their presence in international tournaments brought a sense of excitement and anticipation, with fans eager to see how they would perform on the world stage.

As they established their dominance in football, Messi and Ronaldo began to shape their legacies not only as phenomenal players but also as ambassadors of the sport. Their dedication to football, their relentless pursuit of success, and their ability to inspire those around them set them apart. They were no longer just players; they were symbols of excellence in sport.

As their careers progressed, Lionel Messi and Cristiano Ronaldo not only maintained their high standards but also adapted and evolved, continuing to amass an impressive array of accolades and solidifying their status as legends of the game.

Lionel Messi's role at Barcelona underwent several evolutions as he adapted to different tactical setups and managerial philosophies. Under coaches like Luis Enrique and later Ernesto Valverde, Messi continued to be the linchpin of the Barcelona team. His versatility allowed him to play various roles, from a false nine to a right winger, and even as a playmaker deeper in midfield. Messi's ability to adapt and excel in different positions demonstrated his comprehensive understanding of the game. His list of achievements continued to grow, with numerous La Liga titles, Copa del Rey victories, and continued success in the UEFA Champions League. Individually, Messi kept breaking records, including surpassing Gerd Müller's record for most goals in a calendar year and becoming Barcelona's all-time top scorer.

Cristiano Ronaldo's tenure at Real Madrid was marked by his transformation into one of the most lethal goal-scorers in football history. His goal-scoring prowess was a key factor in Real

Madrid's domestic and European successes, particularly in the Champions League. Ronaldo's ability to deliver in crucial moments was unparalleled, as evidenced by his numerous match-winning performances in the knockout stages of the Champions League. During his time at Real Madrid, Ronaldo secured his status as a Real Madrid legend, breaking numerous records, including becoming the club's all-time top goal-scorer. His individual accolades continued to stack up, with multiple Ballon d'Or titles and numerous other personal honors.

The impact of Messi and Ronaldo extended beyond the trophies they won and the records they broke. They were instrumental in defining the styles and successes of their teams. Their influence was seen in the way Barcelona and Real Madrid played, with both teams often built around their unique talents.

Beyond their club careers, Messi and Ronaldo's influence in the world of football was immense. They were more than just players; they were global icons. Their rivalry, individual achievements, and the way they pushed each other to new heights captivated football fans around the world. They were not only ambassadors for their clubs but also for the sport itself, inspiring a new generation of players and setting new standards in football excellence.

As this chapter concludes, Messi and Ronaldo had firmly established themselves not just as the best players of their generation, but also as two of the greatest footballers in history. Their journey from talented youngsters to dominant forces in football was marked by relentless hard work, adaptation, and an unwavering desire to be the best.

CHAPTER 5: INTERNATIONAL CAREERS

"I thank God every day that Messi is Argentinian." - Diego Maradona

The journeys of Lionel Messi and Cristiano Ronaldo with their national teams stand in contrast to their club careers, marked by moments of both triumph and challenge. This chapter delves into their roles with the Argentine and Portuguese national teams, respectively, and their experiences in major international tournaments.

Lionel Messi's early success at the international level was marked by victories in the FIFA World Youth Championship in 2005 and an Olympic gold medal in 2008. Despite these early triumphs, senior-level success initially eluded him. Messi faced criticism for not replicating his Barcelona form with Argentina, but his commitment to the national team was unwavering. His leadership and influence were particularly evident in Argentina's runs to the finals of the 2014 FIFA World Cup and the 2015 and 2016 Copa Americas, though they ended in heartbreak.

Cristiano Ronaldo's journey with Portugal has been a blend of individual brilliance and team leadership. His role in Portugal's 2004 UEFA European Championship run, where they finished as runners-up, was a sign of things to come. Ronaldo's defining moment came in the 2016 UEFA European Championship, where he led Portugal to their first major international trophy, despite an injury in the final against France.

Both players have faced unique challenges at the international level, with Messi often compared to the legendary Diego Maradona and Ronaldo shouldering the hopes of a nation with fewer footballing accolades.

Lionel Messi's quest for an elusive major trophy with Argentina reached its climax with the 2021 Copa América. Leading Argentina to the title, Messi's performances were instrumental throughout the tournament, and he was named the player of the tournament. This victory was a significant moment in Messi's career, validating his status as a national hero.

Ronaldo's international career saw further success after the 2016 European Championship. In the 2018 FIFA World Cup, he had a memorable tournament, including a hat-trick against Spain. Ronaldo continued to be a crucial figure for Portugal, exemplifying his leadership and goal-scoring prowess.

The UEFA Nations League 2018-2019 saw Ronaldo add another international trophy to his cabinet, reinforcing his crucial role in Portugal's international successes. Ronaldo's ability to perform consistently at a high level in international tournaments, despite the advancing years, highlighted his remarkable longevity and adaptability.

Both Messi and Ronaldo's international careers have been about more than just chasing trophies. They have represented their countries with pride and passion, becoming symbols of national identity.

The 2022 FIFA World Cup in Qatar was a historic event for Lionel Messi. He led Argentina to glory, playing a pivotal role throughout the tournament and scoring in every round. In a thrilling final against France, Messi scored twice, and the match went to a penalty shoot-out, with Argentina emerging victorious. Messi received the Golden Ball for the player of the tournament and finished second in the Golden Boot race. This World Cup victory, ending Argentina's 36-year wait for the trophy, was a crowning achievement in Messi's illustrious career.

Ronaldo's pursuit of World Cup success with Portugal, while not yielding a trophy, has been marked by moments of brilliance and leadership. His performances in World Cups, notably in 2018, have solidified his status as one of the greatest players in the sport.

Both Messi and Ronaldo's international careers have been defined by their ability to inspire their teams and lead by example. Their commitment to representing their countries and their performances on the world stage have made them beloved figures in their nations and respected opponents globally.

In summary, Lionel Messi and Cristiano Ronaldo's international careers have been integral to their legacies as football icons. Messi's triumphs in the Copa América and the FIFA World Cup, coupled with his Olympic success, complete a remarkable journey with the Argentine national team. Cristiano Ronaldo's leadership and crucial role in Portugal's European Championship victory and the UEFA Nations League have solidified his status as a national hero.

Their roles in their national teams have evolved from young talents to seasoned leaders. Messi and Ronaldo have carried the hopes of their nations, often being the focal point of their teams' strategies. Their influence extends beyond their on-field performances; they are leaders who have inspired a generation of footballers and fans alike.

Both players have faced challenges and criticisms on the international stage, but their resilience, commitment, and achievements have been a testament to their greatness, not just as footballers but as ambassadors of the sport.

CHAPTER 6: GOLDEN YEARS: TRIUMPHS AND RECORDS

"There are two things I don't like: losing and drawing"

– Cristiano Ronaldo

As Lionel Messi and Cristiano Ronaldo entered the prime of their careers, they not only continued their dominance in club football but also set new benchmarks in the sport. This chapter explores their season-by-season triumphs, the evolution of their playing styles, and their performances in key matches and tournaments.

Lionel Messi's 2021–2022 season was a period of significant triumphs. In June 2021, he played a pivotal role in Argentina's Copa América victory, their first major title since 1993 and Messi's first major international trophy. His direct involvement in nine of Argentina's twelve goals, scoring four and assisting five, showcased his unparalleled influence on the team. This victory marked a new high in Messi's career, fulfilling his long-standing ambition to win a major title with his national team.

At the 2022 FIFA World Cup in Qatar, Messi led Argentina with exceptional skill and leadership. He scored in every round of the tournament, a first since the introduction of the last-16 round in 1986. In a dramatic and widely acclaimed final against France, Messi scored twice, and the match went to a penalty shoot-out, with Argentina emerging victorious. His performance earned him the Golden Ball for the tournament's best player, becoming the first player to win it twice. He finished second in the Golden Boot race with seven goals, further cementing his legacy as one of the greatest footballers of all time.

Cristiano Ronaldo, during these years, continued to showcase his incredible athleticism and goal-scoring ability. His time at Juventus was marked by consistent performances in Serie A and the Champions League. Ronaldo's ability to adapt to a new league and team underscored his versatility and commitment to excellence. His tenure at Juventus added to his already impressive list of club achievements, including multiple Serie A titles and individual accolades.

Both Messi and Ronaldo's playing styles evolved during these years. Messi, known for his extraordinary dribbling and playmaking abilities, began to take on a deeper role, orchestrating play and contributing to both goal-scoring and creating opportunities for his teammates. His vision and understanding of the game allowed him to influence matches from various positions on the pitch.

Ronaldo's evolution saw him become even more of a clinical finisher. His physicality, aerial ability, and sharp shooting skills made him a constant threat in front of goal. Ronaldo's work ethic and dedication to maintaining his physical condition allowed him to continue performing at an elite level, despite the advancing years.

he golden years of Lionel Messi and Cristiano Ronaldo were not just defined by their club achievements but also by their spectacular performances in key matches and their evolving playing styles, which set new standards in football.

Lionel Messi's performances in crucial matches during this period were a blend of creativity, skill, and decisive goal-scoring. His ability to turn games around with individual brilliance was unmatched. Messi's style evolved as he took on more of a playmaking role, combining his natural dribbling ability with an extraordinary vision for passing and creating opportunities for his teammates. His performance in the 2022 FIFA World Cup final is a testament to his enduring quality and clutch performance ability, scoring key goals and leading Argentina to a long-awaited World Cup triumph.

Cristiano Ronaldo's key performances during these years continued to highlight his status as one of the greatest goal-scorers in the history of the sport. His ability to deliver in high-pressure situations, particularly in the UEFA Champions League, was remarkable. Ronaldo's playing style evolved to focus more on his positioning and finishing ability. His physical attributes, combined with his tactical understanding, allowed him to find spaces and opportunities to score, even as the style of play at Juventus differed from that at Real Madrid.

Both Messi and Ronaldo continued to break records and accumulate individual accolades during this period. Their rivalry, still one of the most talked-about topics in football, pushed them to maintain high levels of performance. They not only competed for titles and awards but also for the unofficial title of the world's best player.

Their influence on their respective teams was profound. Messi's role at Barcelona, and later at Paris Saint-Germain, was central to their attacking play, while Ronaldo's contributions at Juventus and then back at Manchester United were crucial to their successes. Their presence on the pitch elevated the performance of their teams, and their leadership, both on and off the field, was a source of inspiration for teammates and fans alike.

As Lionel Messi and Cristiano Ronaldo continued their careers into the late 2010s and early 2020s, their playing styles kept evolving, adapting to their changing roles in their respective teams and their physical attributes.

Lionel Messi, known for his extraordinary dribbling skills and goal-scoring ability, began to take on a more holistic role in his teams. At Barcelona, and later at Paris Saint-Germain, Messi's playmaking abilities came to the fore. His vision, passing, and ability to dictate the tempo of the game became as influential as his goal-scoring. Messi's adaptability allowed him to remain a crucial part of the team dynamics, contributing not just in goals but in shaping the overall attacking strategy.

Cristiano Ronaldo's evolution saw a focus on maximizing his incredible goal-scoring ability. At

Juventus and upon his return to Manchester United, Ronaldo's play was characterized by intelligent positioning, lethal finishing, and capitalizing on scoring opportunities. His physical prowess, aerial ability, and sheer determination continued to make him one of the most feared forwards in the world.

A comparative analysis of their performances in significant tournaments and clashes reveals both similarities and differences. Both players have had moments of brilliance that have turned the tide in crucial matches. Their ability to perform under pressure has been a hallmark of their careers. In terms of style, Messi's play has often been about weaving magic with the ball, creating chances out of seemingly impossible situations. Ronaldo's approach has been more about power, precision, and effectiveness in front of goal.

In major tournaments, both players have had their share of memorable performances. Messi's leadership and skill were critical in Argentina's Copa América victory and their triumphant 2022 World Cup campaign. Ronaldo's crucial goals and leadership were instrumental in Portugal's Euro 2016 win and their success in the 2018-2019 UEFA Nations League.

Their impact on football during these golden years goes beyond the trophies and accolades. Messi and Ronaldo have inspired a generation of footballers and fans with their dedication, skill, and passion for the game. They have set new standards in football, pushing each other and their teams to achieve greater heights.

Lionel Messi and Cristiano Ronaldo, through their golden years, not only continued to amass incredible achievements but also solidified their legacies as two of the greatest players in the history of football. This final part of the chapter reflects on their enduring impact on the sport, their influence on fans and upcoming players, and the indelible mark they have left on football.

The legacies of Messi and Ronaldo in club football are characterized by their record-breaking performances, consistent excellence, and the transformational impact they had on their teams. Messi's time at Barcelona and later at Paris Saint-Germain saw him set numerous records, including being the all-time top scorer for Barcelona. His style of play, combining mesmerizing dribbling, pinpoint passing, and clinical finishing, redefined the role of a forward. At PSG, Messi continued to demonstrate his versatility and brilliance, adapting to a new league and team dynamics.

Ronaldo's legacy in club football is equally impressive. His tenure at Manchester United, Real Madrid, and Juventus was marked by goal-scoring records, individual accolades, and key contributions to team successes. Ronaldo's physicality, goal-scoring instincts, and ability to perform in crucial moments made him a defining figure in modern football. His return to Manchester United further exemplified his enduring appeal and impact.

Internationally, both Messi and Ronaldo have left a lasting legacy. Messi's triumphs with Argentina in the Copa América and the FIFA World Cup placed him among the greatest national heroes in Argentine sports history. His journey with the national team, from early disappointments to ultimate glory, is a story of resilience and perseverance.

Ronaldo's role in bringing Portugal its first major international trophy in the 2016 UEFA European Championship and his contributions in other tournaments have cemented his status as a national icon. His leadership, both on and off the field, has been instrumental in Portugal's rise as a competitive force in international football.

Beyond their achievements, Messi and Ronaldo have had a profound impact on fans and young players around the world. They have inspired countless individuals with their dedication, work ethic, and passion for the game. Their rivalry, marked by respect and the drive to excel, has captivated football fans, bringing excitement and a higher level of interest in the sport.

Messi and Ronaldo's influence extends beyond the records and trophies. They have redefined what it means to be a successful footballer, combining talent with hard work and a relentless pursuit of excellence. Their stories, from humble beginnings to becoming icons of the sport, serve as an inspiration for future generations.

As this chapter concludes, the legacies of Lionel Messi and Cristiano Ronaldo stand as a testament to their extraordinary careers. They have not only left an indelible mark on football but have also elevated the sport to new heights, setting a benchmark for future generations.

CHAPTER 7: ICONIC MATCHES AND RIVALRIES

"I'm happy with a ball at my feet. My motivation comes from playing the game I love." - Lionel Messi

When Lionel Messi and Cristiano Ronaldo faced each other, the whole world watched. Their encounters were not just football matches; they were historical events in the sport.

One of the most memorable of these direct encounters was the 2011 UEFA Champions League semi-final between Messi's Barcelona and Ronaldo's Real Madrid. The first leg at the

Santiago Bernabéu was a masterclass from Messi. He scored two stunning goals, including a mesmerizing solo effort where he dribbled past several Madrid defenders before slotting the ball past the goalkeeper. This performance was a vivid illustration of Messi's incredible skill and composure under pressure.

Ronaldo, in the same match, showcased his relentless drive and physical prowess. His powerful runs and shots on goal kept the Barcelona defense on constant alert. Although he didn't score in this match, his presence was always a threat, and he played a key role in Madrid's attacking plays.

Their rivalry in La Liga also provided numerous unforgettable moments. The 2012-2013 season saw both players at the peak of their powers, trading goals and victories in their league encounters. In one notable match at Camp Nou, Ronaldo scored a brace, demonstrating his clinical finishing and aerial ability. Messi responded with two goals of his own, including a superbly taken free-kick, underlining his status as one of the best set-piece takers in the game.

These direct duels were more than just personal battles; they were a showcase of their leadership and ability to inspire their teams. Whether it was Messi's quick dribbling and playmaking or Ronaldo's speed and finishing, their performances often dictated the flow and outcome of the games.

Their rivalry extended beyond the pitch, capturing the attention of media and fans worldwide. Each encounter was analyzed and discussed, with every goal, assist, and piece of skill adding to the lore of their competition. It was a rivalry that transcended football, becoming a part of popular culture.

As Messi and Ronaldo continued to face each other over the years, their respect for one another grew. They pushed each other to greater heights, acknowledging the other's talent and achievements. Their rivalry was a testament to their commitment to excellence and their undying passion for the game.

The matches between Messi and Ronaldo will forever be etched in the annals of football history. They were not just games; they were epic battles between two of the greatest players the sport has ever seen. Players who, through their rivalry, changed football forever.

The rivalry between Lionel Messi and Cristiano Ronaldo also shone brightly in domestic cup competitions. In the 2011 Copa del Rey final, a spectacular header from Ronaldo in extra time secured victory for Real Madrid. This goal was a testament to Ronaldo's physicality and his ability to deliver in crucial moments. The match was a tense affair, with both players exerting significant influence, but it was Ronaldo's decisive moment that clinched the trophy for Madrid.

In contrast, during the 2012 Supercopa de España, Messi demonstrated his own clutch ability. He scored key goals in both legs of the tie, including a brilliant free-kick in the second leg at the Santiago Bernabéu. His performance was a crucial factor in Barcelona lifting the trophy, highlighting his role as a game-changer for his team.

These iconic matchups were not just about the goals they scored but also about their influence on the pitch. Messi, with his vision and creativity, often dictated the pace and rhythm of Barcelona's play, while Ronaldo's athleticism and killer instinct kept opposing defenses on edge.

The 2015-2016 season brought another memorable chapter to their rivalry. In a highly anticipated league match at the Camp Nou, both players were at their best. Ronaldo scored a late winner, silencing the home crowd with a display of his trademark speed and finishing. Messi, though not on the scoresheet, was a constant threat throughout the game, weaving through Madrid's defense with his signature dribbling.

Their encounters were a blend of artistry and athleticism, each player bringing their unique style to the forefront. Messi's low center of gravity and close ball control contrasted with Ronaldo's physical presence and aerial prowess. These differences only added to the spectacle, making each encounter unpredictable and exhilarating.

Off the field, the rivalry between Messi and Ronaldo was equally compelling. Their competition for individual awards, particularly the Ballon d'Or, was a yearly highlight. Each player's success seemed to drive the other to greater heights, setting new records and redefining the standards of excellence in football.

As the years passed, their rivalry evolved from fierce competition to mutual admiration. The respect they had for each other was evident in their public statements and gestures on the field. They recognized that their rivalry was not just about personal glory, but about pushing each other and the sport to new levels.

Messi and Ronaldo's direct duels will be remembered as some of the greatest moments in football history. Their rivalry was a spectacle of skill, determination, and passion, captivating fans around the world. It was a rivalry that went beyond goals and trophies, embodying the spirit of competition and the love for the beautiful game.

As their careers progressed, the Messi-Ronaldo rivalry became a yardstick for footballing greatness. Each season, their encounters in various competitions were highly anticipated events, not just for their fans but for football enthusiasts worldwide.

The 2017-2018 season brought another memorable encounter in the Spanish Super Cup. Barcelona and Real Madrid faced off in a fiercely contested two-legged affair. Ronaldo's stunning goal in the first leg at Camp Nou was a display of raw power and precision. However, he was sent off shortly after, adding drama to an already intense match. Messi, on the other hand, was a constant creative force, orchestrating

Barcelona's attacks and scoring a penalty in the same match. Despite his efforts, Real Madrid emerged victorious, showcasing the depth of their rivalry.

Their battles in the Champions League also provided moments of high drama. In the 2010-2011 season, they met in the semi-finals, with Barcelona coming out on top. Messi was instrumental in this victory, scoring two goals in the first leg. These goals were a showcase of his exceptional talent, cementing his place as one of the key players in Barcelona's European dominance.

Ronaldo's move to Juventus in 2018 opened a new chapter in their rivalry. While direct encounters became less frequent, their competition continued on the European stage and in the race for individual awards. Ronaldo's adaptation to the Italian league and his continued goal-scoring exploits were a testament to his enduring quality and adaptability.

Even as they entered the latter stages of their careers, Messi and Ronaldo continued to astonish the football world with their performances. Their ability to maintain such high standards over a prolonged period is a testament to their dedication, professionalism, and sheer love for the game.

The rivalry between Messi and Ronaldo has been more than just a series of matches. It has been a narrative of two extraordinary careers intertwined, each pushing the other to greater heights. They have not only defined an era in football but have also set the benchmark for future generations.

Their direct duels, full of memorable goals, breathtaking skills, and intense competition, will be cherished by football fans for years to come. Messi and Ronaldo have not just been competitors; they have been protagonists in a football story for the ages, a story of rivalry, respect, and remarkable talent.

As we look back on the iconic matches and rivalries that defined their careers, it is clear that Messi and Ronaldo have left an indelible mark on the world of football. Their legacy is not just in the records they broke or the trophies they won, but in the moments of magic they created on the pitch, captivating millions around the globe.

CHAPTER 8: TRANSITIONS AND ADAPTATIONS

"My life is a challenge, and I like challenges." – Cristiano Ronaldo

Cristiano Ronaldo's journey through the football world has been a narrative of constant adaptation and evolution. From his early days at Sporting CP, where he first showcased his raw talent and remarkable dribbling skills, Ronaldo rapidly ascended the ranks of footballing greats. At age 16, he made a remarkable leap, playing for Sporting's under-16, under-17, under-18 teams, the B team, and the first team in a single season, a testament to his prodigious talent.

His debut for Sporting CP's senior team in a UEFA Champions League qualifying round against Inter Milan on 14 August 2002 marked the beginning of an illustrious senior career. Ronaldo's performances for Sporting CP, particularly in a match against Manchester United, caught the eye of United's manager, Alex Ferguson, who was determined to acquire him. The transfer to Manchester United in 2003 for £12.24 million was a pivotal moment, making Ronaldo the first Portuguese player to sign for the club.

At Manchester United, Ronaldo's development and breakthrough were phenomenal. His debut against Bolton Wanderers in the Premier League was met with a standing ovation, and his first season was marked by scintillating performances and his first trophy, the 2004 FA Ronaldo's time at United was a blend of personal growth and collective success. He developed a reputation for his footwork, speed, and goal-scoring prowess. His remarkable ability to adapt and improve was evident in his evolution from a flashy winger to a prolific goal-scorer.

In 2009, Ronaldo made a record-breaking move to Real Madrid for €94 million, becoming a key contributor to the team's success, including four Champions League titles. His time at Real Madrid was marked by incredible goal-scoring feats and numerous individual awards, including multiple Ballon d'Or wins.

Ronaldo's adaptability was further tested with his transfer to Juventus in 2018. At Juventus, he continued to defy expectations, becoming the first player to win league titles in England, Spain, and Italy. His ability to adjust to different leagues and teams while maintaining his high standards is a testament to his extraordinary talent and work ethic.

In 2023, Ronaldo made a surprising move to Al Nassr in Saudi Arabia, marking another chapter in his illustrious career. This move, although unexpected, underscores Ronaldo's willingness to embrace new challenges and experiences in his football journey.

Ronaldo's career is a story of continuous transitions and adaptations, rising to challenges in different leagues and teams. His journey reflects his ability to evolve and succeed in varying environments, solidifying his status as one of football's all-time greats.

Lionel Messi's career at Barcelona has been a remarkable journey of evolution and adaptability. From his debut as a diminutive yet immensely talented teenager to becoming the heart and soul of one of the world's most prestigious football clubs, Messi's time at Barcelona is a tale of extraordinary growth and change.

Messi's early years at Barcelona were marked by rapid development under the guidance of coaches like Frank Rijkaard and later Pep Guardiola. Under Rijkaard, Messi began to show glimpses of his future brilliance, playing an integral role in the team's 2005-2006 Champions League triumph. However, it was under Guardiola's tenure that Messi truly flourished, transforming into one of the most lethal forwards in the game.

Guardiola's Barcelona, known for its tiki-taka style of play, was the perfect environment for Messi to showcase his unique abilities. His close ball control, vision, and incredible dribbling skills were complemented by a newfound goal-scoring prowess. The 2008-2009 season was a standout, with Messi scoring 38 goals in all competitions and playing a pivotal role in Barcelona's historic treble, winning La Liga, Copa del Rey, and the Champions League.

Messi's adaptability was further tested with the arrival of Luis Enrique as coach in 2014. Under Enrique, Messi's role evolved to accommodate the attacking prowess of Neymar and Luis Suárez. This adaptation saw Messi taking on more of a playmaker role, demonstrating his versatility and team-first approach. The 2014-2015 season culminated in another treble for Barcelona, with Messi contributing 58 goals across all competitions.

Messi's ability to adapt to different tactical systems and coaches was evident throughout his time at Barcelona. Whether it was playing on the right wing, as a false nine, or even dropping deeper into midfield, Messi consistently found ways to impact games. His understanding of the game, combined with his technical skills, made him a formidable force, regardless of the tactical setup.

Beyond his adaptability on the pitch, Messi's leadership at Barcelona evolved over the years. Initially a quiet and reserved figure, Messi grew into a leader, often wearing the captain's armband and inspiring his teammates through his performances and work ethic. His dedication to Barcelona was evident in his loyalty to the club, remaining a one-club man for the majority of his career.

In 2021, in a turn of events that shocked the football world, Messi left Barcelona to join Paris Saint-Germain. This move marked a new chapter in his career, challenging him to adapt to a new league, team, and cultural environment. His transfer to PSG was not just a change of clubs but a testament to his enduring ambition and desire to excel at the highest level.

Lionel Messi's journey at Barcelona and beyond is a testament to his incredible ability to adapt and excel in the ever-changing world of football. His evolution from a young talent to a global icon is a story of adaptability, resilience, and unparalleled skill, solidifying his status as one of the game's greatest players.

Lionel Messi's move to Paris Saint-Germain (PSG) in 2021 marked a significant milestone in his illustrious career. After spending more than two decades at Barcelona, where he became synonymous with the club's identity, Messi's transition to a new league and team was a momentous event in world football.

At PSG, Messi was reunited with former Barcelona teammate Neymar and joined forces with Kylian Mbappé, forming one of the most formidable attacking trios in the sport's history. This new chapter challenged Messi to adapt not only to a new team and league but also to a new country and culture.

The Ligue 1, France's top football league, presented a different style of play compared to La Liga. Known for its physicality and pace, Ligue 1 required Messi to adjust his game. Despite these challenges, Messi's class was immediately evident. His vision, creativity, and exceptional technical skills translated seamlessly to the French league.

Messi's first season at PSG was marked by memorable moments and milestones. He scored his first goal for PSG in a Champions League match against Manchester City, showcasing his enduring quality against top European competition. In Ligue 1, Messi's playmaking abilities shone, as he adapted to become more of a creator, utilizing his unparalleled vision and passing skills to set up goals.

One of the highlights of Messi's time at PSG was his performance in the Champions League. His experience and skill in Europe's elite competition were invaluable to PSG's ambitions. Messi's ability to perform on the biggest stage, against the toughest opponents, remained undiminished, as he continued to be a key player in crucial matches.

Messi's adaptation to PSG also showcased his professionalism and work ethic. Despite the initial challenges of moving to a new team and league, Messi remained committed to his craft, working tirelessly to integrate into PSG's system and style of play. His attitude and dedication were a testament to his character and his relentless pursuit of excellence.

Off the field, Messi's impact at PSG extended beyond the pitch. His arrival brought a new level of global attention to the club and the French league. Messi's presence at PSG not only elevated the team's profile but also contributed to the growth and popularity of Ligue 1 worldwide.

In summary, Lionel Messi's transition to PSG has been another remarkable chapter in his career. His ability to adapt to new challenges and maintain his high standards at one of Europe's top clubs is a further demonstration of his extraordinary talent and legacy in football. As Messi continues to write his story at PSG and beyond, his journey remains a captivating tale of adaptability, resilience, and unparalleled footballing brilliance.

Lionel Messi's transition to Paris Saint-Germain (PSG) in 2021 marked a significant change in his storied career. After more than two decades at Barcelona, Messi's move to PSG was a bold step into a new league and a different footballing culture. At PSG, Messi continued to display his extraordinary skills, contributing significantly to the team's success in the domestic league and the Champions League.

However, the most notable chapter in Messi's career post-PSG was his move to Major League Soccer (MLS) in the United States. In 2023, Messi joined Inter Miami, a move that sent ripples across the footballing world. This transfer was not just about playing in a new league but also about expanding his influence in a growing football market.

At Inter Miami, Messi's impact was immediate and profound. His presence boosted the team's performance, and his leadership on and off the field was instrumental in their success. Messi's skill, vision, and creativity shone brightly in MLS, where he adapted seamlessly to the style of play and became a pivotal player for his team.

The highlight of Messi's time at Inter Miami came in August 2023, when he led the team to victory in the Leagues Cup, a testament to his continued excellence and ability to make a significant impact in different football environments.

Moreover, in October 2023, Messi achieved yet another milestone by winning the Ballon d'Or award for a record-breaking eighth time. This accolade was a recognition of his enduring brilliance and his remarkable adaptability across different leagues and stages of his career.

Lionel Messi's journey from Barcelona to PSG and then to Inter Miami exemplifies his remarkable ability to adapt and excel, regardless of the circumstances. His transitions between clubs and leagues highlight his versatility, resilience, and unwavering commitment to excellence. Messi's career is a story of continuous growth, adaptation, and an undying passion for the game, cementing his status as one of the greatest players in the history of football.

CHAPTER 9: BEYOND FOOTBALL

"Being a bit famous now gives me the opportunity to help people who really need it, especially children." - Lionel Messi

The phenomenal success of Lionel Messi and Cristiano Ronaldo has made them two of the most famous and influential sports stars on the planet. Their impact stretches far beyond the pitch and into the realms of global culture, business, philanthropy, and media.

In terms of global cultural influence, both players are revered sports icons with legions of passionate fans. Ronaldo and Messi replicas shirts and merchandise sell in enormous volumes, making them not just household names in football but also recognizable celebrities around the world. Both are national heroes and de facto ambassadors for their home countries. Young fans in parks and streets across the world emulate their playing styles, goal celebrations and on-pitch personas. The sheer inspiration they provide to aspiring footballers cannot be understated.

Ronaldo and Messi have become archetypes of the modern, successful sports superstar. Their fame, fueled by their exploits and achievements, has enabled them to land lucrative endorsement deals with blue-chip companies including Nike,

Adidas, Emirates Airlines, and Samsung. They have fronted major international advertising campaigns that have expanded their visibility beyond football. Both players have become brands unto themselves - CR7 and Messi being instantly identifiable symbols. Their social media presence reflects their cultural influence - Ronaldo has over half a billion followers across platforms, while Messi has over 300 million. These staggering numbers put them among the most followed public figures in the world.

Lionel Messi and Cristiano Ronaldo have not just stopped at being global icons - they have actively leveraged their sporting success for positive social impact. Both players are involved extensively with charity work and philanthropy.

Ronaldo has served as a goodwill ambassador for several important charitable causes during his career. He has supported Save the Children for over a decade, raising funds and awareness for child hunger and education. Through his namesake foundation, Ronaldo has donated millions towards disaster relief, fighting poverty, and providing healthcare access to those in need.

Messi has been a UNICEF goodwill ambassador since 2010. He has promoted children's rights and lobbied for equity in access to education, healthcare and protection. Messi has also provided financial contributions and raised funds for medical care for disadvantaged children in Argentina and Spain. His sincere involvement in these charitable efforts has earned him respect beyond his sporting brilliance.

Both Ronaldo and Messi have effectively used their fame and resources to champion social causes and enact positive change. While they are fierce individual competitors on the pitch, they have worked together to participate in charity friendlies such as the Match Against Poverty organized by the United Nations. Their shared spirit of generosity reflects an understanding that their sporting impact can extend beyond the boundaries of the football pitch.

The fame and success of Lionel Messi and Cristiano Ronaldo has also brought increased media scrutiny and coverage of their lives on and off the field. Their exploits and achievements are chronicled 24/7 by sports media around the world. With modern media's insatiable appetite for celebrity news, coverage also extends into their personal lives.

This level of scrutiny has provided challenges for both players. Media narratives comparing them have often simplified their playing styles and careers into reductive binaries - Ronaldo the athletic specimen vs the diminutive, naturally gifted Messi. Both have faced intense criticism at times from pundits and fans. Ronaldo's perceived selfishness and Messi's struggles with his national team have been constant fixtures in media discourse.

Off the field, both players have faced allegations around tax avoidance and probes into their finances and business dealings. These incidents have presented PR challenges but also opportunities for them to rehabilitate their reputations via carefully tailored media interactions. Their public statements and appearances since have positioned them as sober professionals dedicated to excelling in their craft.

Amidst the noise, both players have won media praise for their sportsmanship and conduct. Ronaldo consoling a young, dejected Messi fan won hearts, as did Messi's humility in defeat after Argentina's 2018 World Cup loss. Such moments have reinforced their sporting role model status for millions globally.

In summary, the intense media spotlight on Messi and Ronaldo has provided an additional dimension for them to manage alongside their footballing careers. But through caution and savvy positioning, they have largely succeeded in molding public perception into that of dedicated, charitable professionals setting an example both on and off the pitch.

CHAPTER 10: LIFE OFF-PITCH

"I'm not perfect, but I try to be the best version of myself every day." – Cristiano Ronaldo

While renowned for their exploits on the pitch, Lionel Messi and Cristiano Ronaldo have personal lives, interests and professional pursuits away from football that provide balance and inspiration.

In terms of family, Messi married his longtime partner Antonella Roccuzzo in 2017. They have three sons together - Thiago, Mateo and Ciro. Messi maintains a close-knit family life, crediting Roccuzzo for providing him stability amidst the turbulence of his career. Ronaldo became a father in 2010 when his first son, Cristiano Jr., was born to a surrogate mother. He now has four children - his daughter Alana Martina, and twins, Eva and Mateo born via surrogacy along with Cristiano Jr.

Both players take active interest in their children's development, supporting their sporting activities and keeping them grounded. Ronaldo's son is already making a name for himself in youth football. Both players credit fatherhood with bringing greater maturity, perspective and balance to their lives.

Away from football, Messi enjoys a quiet, lowkey lifestyle centered around family. He often returns to hometown Rosario in Argentina to visit relatives and friends. Messi has indicated his love for activities like playing the guitar, watching television, and enjoying traditional Argentinian barbeque. In contrast, Ronaldo enjoys a more lavish, jetsetting lifestyle, relishing fast cars, expensive real estate and exotic vacations. Despite their different lifestyles, both find sanctuary with family away from the limelight.

Lionel Messi and Cristiano Ronaldo's drive for success has extended into their business activities and investments off the pitch. Their financial power allows them to explore opportunities beyond football.

Ronaldo established his CR7 brand of apparel, footwear and accessories in a partnership with a major U.S. manufacturer. He has also acquired a luxury hotel brand and opened hotels in major cities. Ronaldo leverages his massive social media following for lucrative product endorsements and sponsorships. Reports suggest his current earnings from commercial activities exceed his playing contract.

Messi has created his own clothing line and stores selling Messi-branded apparel around the globe. He has forged multi-million dollar sponsorships with Adidas, Pepsi, Turkish Airlines and other brands. Messi has leveraged his name for profitable real estate developments in Spain.

He has invested in football training centers for youth. Both stars have built business empires by capitalizing on their sporting fame.

These entrepreneurial pursuits have raised their endorsements and total compensation to record levels in sports history. According to Forbes, Ronaldo and Messi were the highest paid athletes in the world for several years in the late 2010s. While financial motivations exist, their off-pitch activities provide them opportunities to continue engaging with sport after retiring as players.

The personal lives of Lionel Messi and Cristiano Ronaldo have occasionally intersected with their professional careers in football. Family situations, relationships and outside interests have at times enhanced or provided challenges to their footballing success.

The biggest impact has come after both settled down as family men following the birth of their children. Fatherhood has brought greater maturity, stability and perspective that allowed them to excel further on the pitch professionally. Their partners have also provided invaluable emotional support through the ups and downs.

However, distractions have emerged at times. Ronaldo has faced accusations around encounter with a woman in a Las Vegas hotel room, leading to legal wrangling. Messi was embroiled in a court case in Spain around alleged tax fraud, though his conviction was later overturned. Both players have faced intense media scrutiny of their private lives at times, forming reputational challenges alongside footballing ones.

On the positive side, their strong family values and interests beyond football - such as Ronaldo's passion for fashion and Messi's love of home cooking - have humanized their personas for the public. Their authentic self-expression and commitment to personal growth enhances their sporting legacy. Overall, their private lives have provided support as well as learning experiences that contributed to their success.

CHAPTER 11: COMPARISON AND CONTRAST

"I never had any problems with my height. I was always the smallest kid, at school and in my teams." - Lionel Messi

The playing styles of Lionel Messi and Cristiano Ronaldo have sparked endless analysis and debate among fans and experts. Their differing approaches to the game are a reflection of their unique talents and footballing philosophies.

In terms of technique, Messi's game is characterized by extraordinary close control, nimble dribbling, and flair. His low center of gravity, quick feet, and ability to change direction rapidly allow him to slalom through defenses with ease. Messi combines his dribbling with preternatural vision, able to thread pinpoint passes between lines of defenders. He is a master of the one-two pass, exchanging quick short passes to unlock defenses. Messi's shooting range is vast, from curled efforts from distance to clinical finishes inside the box with both feet. His style epitomizes natural talent, joy, and expressiveness on the ball.

Ronaldo's game relies more on sheer power, pace, and athleticism. His muscular physique provides the platform for his forceful, direct style. Ronaldo drives powerfully at defenders, barreling past them with strength and speed. His leaping ability makes him a dominant force in the air, excelling at headers. Ronaldo strikes the ball with extraordinary power, especially from long range and on free kicks. His style reflects determination, ambition, and relentless hard work to push his physique and skills to the limit.

In terms of productivity, both Messi and Ronaldo possess staggering statistics. Ronaldo has scored an astonishing 872 senior career goals to date, averaging 0.72 goals per game across his time at Sporting, Manchester United, Real Madrid, Juventus and Portugal. Messi has scored 821 goals in his career so far, with a marginally better goals-per-game ratio of 0.78 across his spells at Barcelona, PSG and with Argentina.

Lionel Messi has an edge over Ronaldo when it comes to creative statistics. He has made 361 assists over the course of his illustrious career, compared to Ronaldo's 249. Messi creates 3.36 chances per 90 minutes, whereas Ronaldo creates 2.34 chances per 90 minutes. Messi's superior passing skills are further reflected in his tally of 450 successful throughballs, nearly six times Ronaldo's 81. Between 2009 and 2022, Messi created 1,393 key passes, 461 more than Ronaldo's 932.

However, Ronaldo's heading and aerial statistics massively exceed Messi's. He has scored 146 headed goals in his career compared to just 26 for Messi. Since 2009, Ronaldo has won 770 aerial duels to Messi's 116, capitalizing on his imposing leap and physique. Ronaldo is also ahead in terms of shooting volume, having attempted 3,637 shots to Messi's 2,941 in league and Champions League matches since 2009. However, Messi is the more efficient shooter, scoring with 12.5% of his shots compared to Ronaldo's 11.1%.

In terms of honours, both players have achieved staggering success. Ronaldo has won a phenomenal 35 trophies across his time at

United, Real Madrid, Juventus and Portugal. Messi has currently won 44 major honours in his spells at Barcelona, PSG and with Argentina. Ronaldo has 5 Champions League winner's medals to Messi's 4. However, Messi has 12 domestic league titles to Ronaldo's 7 league championships.

The extraordinary numbers and honours amassed by Lionel Messi and Cristiano Ronaldo are almost too astonishing to comprehend. They have broken numerous long-standing records over their careers thus far.

Messi's peak statistical year came in 2012 when he scored an otherworldly total of 91 goals for Barcelona and Argentina, including 79 official goals. This demolished Gerd Muller's 40-year-old record of 85 goals in a calendar year. Ronaldo's best goal-scoring year was in 2013, when he scored 69 goals for Real Madrid and Portugal.

In La Liga, Messi holds the record for most goals in a season with 50 in 2011-12 as well as most consecutive matches scored in (21 games). Ronaldo has the Champions League records for most goals (141), most group stage goals (79), most knock-out goals (67) and most hat-tricks (8).

Ronaldo (5) has more Champions League winner's medals than Messi (4), and also holds the record for most goals in the tournament's knockout stage (67). Messi however has the most domestic league titles of the two, with 12 to Ronaldo's 7. In 2022, Messi finally claimed the ultimate prize at international level, leading Argentina to World Cup glory.

Messi has won a record eight FIFA Ballon d'Or awards, compared to five for Ronaldo. Ronaldo holds the record for most goals ever scored for an international team, with 118 goals for Portugal as of December 2022.

In essence, Messi and Ronaldo have broken and rewritten the record books on multiple fronts, setting new standards of excellence in the process. Their careers will go down in football history not just for their honours and achievements, but for their ability to push the boundaries of possibility in the sport.

CHAPTER 12: LEGACY AND CONTINUING INFLUENCE

"The difference between good and great is attention to detail." – Cristiano Ronaldo

The legacies of Lionel Messi and Cristiano Ronaldo will endure long after they hang up their boots. Their impact on football, and their influence on upcoming generations, has been profound and will continue shaping the sport for years to come.

Both players have redefined the art of forward play, setting new standards that future footballers will aspire towards. Messi has embodied the fluid, naturally gifted attacker, who can both score and create beautifully. His trademark dribbling style, vision, and imaginative play will inspire young players for decades. Ronaldo's dedication to honing his physique and skills has shown what levels athletes can push themselves to with determination. His power, work ethic and lethal finishing will motivate strikers around the world.

 Tactically, Messi and Ronaldo forced coaches to adapt systems to get the best out of them. Guardiola's Barcelona side, with its fluid positioning and emphasis on control, brought the best out of Messi's playmaking abilities. Real Madrid developed fast-paced counter-attacking tactics to weaponize Ronaldo's pace and directness. Their dominance has reshaped tactical trends in the sport.

Both players have transcended football to become global icons. Their popularity, reinforced through endorsements, social media and pop culture, has expanded football's reach beyond dedicated fans. Messi and Ronaldo are household names, even to casual followers or non-football enthusiasts. Their influence ensures football's profile will remain strong for the foreseeable future.

As ambassadors, Lionel Messi and Cristiano Ronaldo have been invaluable for promoting the positive values of football globally. They are the shining examples of how talent and hard work can lead to unimaginable success. Their professionalism, work ethic and competitive spirit on the pitch have shown what it takes to reach the pinnacle of sport.

The Messi vs Ronaldo rivalry has captured imaginations not just because of its sporting significance, but also for the respect and sportsmanship that exists between them. Despite the intensity of their rivalry, there is a clear mutual admiration between the two modern legends. Their rivalry has been an example of positive competition pushing both to unprecedented heights.

Both players have used their powerful platforms for social initiatives, supporting charitable causes and giving back to communities. Ronaldo and Messi have been conscientious role models for young fans, motivating them to work hard academically and in sport. Their careers have shown that becoming a well-rounded person is as important as excelling professionally.

As the final acts of their careers approach, both Messi and Ronaldo have ensured their legacies in football will be everlasting. They have not just conquered the record books but also made an imprint on football culture and imagination worldwide. Their influence will continue inspiring dreams and fanning passion for the beautiful game for decades to come.

CHAPTER 13: CONCLUSION

"Some may compare us, but we are simply two players who love the game and try to give our best." - Lionel Messi on Ronaldo

"He is a phenomenon, and I truly admire the career he has built. Football wouldn't be the same without him." - Cristiano Ronaldo on Messi

Lionel Messi and Cristiano Ronaldo's football journeys have enthralled fans for over a decade and a half. Their larger-than-life careers have reshaped the sport in many ways, setting new benchmarks both on and off the pitch. Their rivalry will go down as one of the most compelling in sporting history, two supreme yet contrasting talents driving each other to unprecedented heights.

Looking back, their list of records, trophies and individual honors seems scarcely believable. Between them they have won 13 FIFA Ballon d'Or awards, over 50 domestic league titles, 9 UEFA Champions Leagues, multiple continental championships and cups. Both have broken goal-scoring and appearance records for their clubs and countries. Their consistency and longevity at the highest echelons of football are unparalleled.

Beyond mere statistics and silverware, Messi and Ronaldo's legacy is one of pushing the boundaries of excellence and possibility in sport. Their dedication, work ethic and undying passion for football have made them transcendent superstars. They have set the bar higher for every aspect of an elite football career, from training to nutrition, mental strength to leadership.

Messi and Ronaldo's styles, though different, will both profoundly inspire future generations. Messi's artistry, close control and fluidity epitomize natural talent. Ronaldo's power, drive and lethal finishing reflect the heights achievable through determination. Both philosophies will continue moulding football's future.

As their legendary journeys enter their final acts, the Messi vs Ronaldo debate will rage on. Fans will continue comparing their stats, dissecting their skills and arguing over who reigns supreme. Their rivalry will be remembered as special not just for pushing them to greater feats, but also for the respect that exists between these two icons. Its legacy will endure through their awe-inspiring achievements and inspiring influence over football.

CHAPTER 14: TRIVIA

Theme 1: Lionel Messi

1. At what age did Messi join FC Barcelona's youth academy, La Masia?
2. What is the name of the growth hormone deficiency Messi was diagnosed with as a child?
3. How many Ballon d'Or awards has Messi won as of 2023?
4. What unique record did Messi set with his 91 goals in the calendar year 2012?
5. Which club did Messi transfer to in 2021?
6. Messi won his first major international trophy with Argentina in what year and competition?
7. What is Messi's full name?
8. Against which team did Messi score his first goal for Barcelona?
9. What is Messi's jersey number for Argentina?
10. Who was Messi's first coach at Barcelona?

Answers:

1. 13 years old.

2. Growth hormone deficiency (GHD).

3. Seven Ballon d'Or awards.

4. Most goals scored in a calendar year.

5. Paris Saint-Germain (PSG).

6. 2021, Copa America.

7. Lionel Andrés Messi.

8. Albacete.

9. Number 10.

10. Frank Rijkaard.

Theme 2: Cristiano Ronaldo

1. Ronaldo's famous "SIUUU" celebration was first done in what year?
2. What was Ronaldo's jersey number at Sporting CP?
3. How many UEFA Champions League titles has Ronaldo won?
4. Ronaldo began his career with which Portuguese club?
5. What record did Ronaldo set with his transfer from Manchester United to Real Madrid in 2009?
6. Ronaldo scored his 100th international goal for Portugal against which team?
7. At what age did Ronaldo first captain the Portugal national team?
8. Ronaldo won his first Ballon d'Or in which year?
9. Which country was Ronaldo born in?

10. In 2023, which club did Ronaldo transfer to from Manchester United?

Answers:

1. 2013.

2. Number 28.

3. Five UEFA Champions League titles.

4. Sporting CP.

5. The most expensive football transfer at the time.

6. Sweden.

7. 22 years old.

8. 2008.

9. Portugal.

10. Al Nassr.

Theme 3: El Clásico

1. What is El Clásico?
2. In which stadium did the highest-scoring El Clásico take place?
3. Who holds the record for most goals in El Clásico matches?
4. When was the first official El Clásico match played?
5. Which player transferred from Barcelona to Real Madrid in 2000, intensifying the rivalry?
6. How often is El Clásico typically played in a season?
7. Which Real Madrid legend is known for his performances in El Clásico during the 1950s and 1960s?
8. What is the biggest victory margin in an El Clásico match?
9. Who scored the winning goal in the El Clásico of April 2017?

10. What was unique about El Clásico during the Spanish Civil War?

Answers:

1. The football match between FC Barcelona and Real Madrid.
2. Santiago Bernabéu Stadium.
3. Lionel Messi.
4. 1902.
5. Luís Figo.
6. At least twice (excluding other competitions).
7. Alfredo Di Stéfano.
8. 11-1 in favor of Real Madrid.
9. Lionel Messi.
10. It was suspended due to the war.

Theme 4: Major Trophies and Achievements

1. Which player has won the most European Golden Shoes?
2. What is the name of the award given to the best player in a FIFA World Cup?
3. Who won the UEFA Men's Player of the Year Award in 2018?
4. Name the club that won the UEFA Champions League in 2006.
5. What trophy is awarded to the winner of Copa America?
6. Who was the top scorer in the 2006 FIFA World Cup?
7. What is the name of the trophy awarded for winning La Liga?
8. Which team won the UEFA European Championship in 2016?
9. Who holds the record for the most goals in a single Premier League season?

10. Which player won the FIFA Club World Cup Golden Ball in 2011?

Answers:

1. Lionel Messi.

2. The Golden Ball.

3. Luka Modrić.

4. FC Barcelona.

5. Copa America Trophy.

6. Miroslav Klose.

7. The La Liga Trophy.

8. Portugal.

9. Mohamed Salah.

10. Lionel Messi.

Theme 5: Football Records and Milestones

1. Who holds the record for the most goals in UEFA Champions League history?
2. What is the highest number of goals scored by a single player in a FIFA World Cup tournament?
3. Which player has the most appearances in the English Premier League?
4. Name the first player to win league titles in England, Spain, and Italy.
5. What is the record for the longest unbeaten run in the Premier League?
6. Who scored the fastest goal in World Cup history?
7. Which player has won the most FIFA World Player of the Year awards?
8. What is the record for the most consecutive league wins in La Liga?
9. Name the youngest player to captain a team in the UEFA Champions League.

10. Who is the all-time top scorer for the England national team?

Answers:

1. Cristiano Ronaldo.

2. 13 goals (Just Fontaine, 1958).

3. Gareth Barry.

4. Cristiano Ronaldo.

5. 49 matches (Arsenal).

6. Hakan Şükür (11 seconds, 2002).

7. Lionel Messi.

8. 16 wins (Barcelona, 2010-2011).

9. Ruben Neves.

10. Wayne Rooney.

CHAPTER 15: GUESS WHO

#1. A French star in Madrid, with control so neat,

At the heart of the game, he was hard to beat.

With a touch of class, and a head shaved clean,

In the biggest matches, he was often seen.

From Juventus to Real, his legacy grew,

Can you guess who he is, with skills not few?

#2. From Italy he came, with a defensive might,

In Milan he stayed, a true Rossoneri knight.

A captain, a leader, strong and revered,

With him at the back, opponents often feared.

His name echoes in San Siro's halls,

Can you name this legend, who rarely falls?

#3. A Dutch master of the pitch, with vision so clear,

At Barcelona and Ajax, his talent was near.

With passes so sharp, and a tactical mind,

In football's history, his name you'll find.

A creator, a thinker, in midfield he reigned,

Can you name this artist, whose legacy remained?

Answers:

1. Zinedine Zidane

2. Paolo Maldini

3. Johan Cruyff

FOOTY JOKE CORNER

- What did the referee say to the chicken who tripped an opponent? *"That's a fowl!"*
- What's black and white, then black and white, then black and white again? *A Newcastle supporter tumbling down a slope!*
- I left two Everton tickets on my car dashboard yesterday. When I returned, someone had broken the window and left two more.
- Why was the football player sad on his birthday? *He received a red card!*
- What do you call someone who stands between goalposts and stops the ball from escaping? *Annette!*

- England's playing Iceland tomorrow. If they win, they're up against Tesco next week, followed by Asda.
- Which footbal team is a fan of desserts? *Aston Vanilla!*
- Where's the best place in the U.S. to buy a football uniform? *New Jersey!*
- What do Lionel Messi and a magician share in common? *They both can pull off hat-tricks!*
- The new coach of our struggling football team is strict. Last weekend, he caught two fans trying to leave early. He told them, "Get back in there and watch till the end!"
- Why did Cinderella get removed from the football team? *She kept avoiding the ball!*

- What's a goalie's favorite meal? *Beans on the post!*
- Why don't grasshoppers watch football? *They're cricket fans!*
- What's a ghost's preferred football position? *Ghoulkeeper!*
- Why did the coach bring pencils to the locker room before the match? *He was hoping for a draw!*
- Did you hear about the new Everton Bra? *Great support, but no cups!*
- Who was the top scorer in the Greek Mythology League? *The centaur striker!*
- What did the coach do when the field was flooded? *He sent in the subs!*

- My partner broke up with me because of my football obsession. I'm a bit down – we'd been together for three seasons.
- What ship can hold 20 football teams but only three leave each season? The Premier-ship!
- What's the difference between Bournemouth and a tea bag? The tea bag remains in the cup longer!
- Why was the world's best football player told to clean their room? *Because it was Messi!*
- Which part of the football field smells the best? *The scent-er spot!*
- Why did the football ball quit? *It was tired of being kicked around!*

- What do you call a Brentford fan after their team wins the Premier League? *Dreaming!*
- Why aren't football stadiums in space? *Lack of atmosphere!*
- Why do football players remind you of toddlers? *Both love to dribble!*
- God and Satan decided to settle their differences with a football match. God said, "All the good players come to heaven." Satan smirked, "But we have all the referees."
- Which football team has their tactics down? *The Hammers.*
- Why did the football player hold his shoe to his ear? *He loved sole tunes!*

- What's the coldest stadium in the Premiership? *Icy Trafford!*
- Which team begins every match with energy? *The Gunners!*
- What runs around the football field but never moves? *The sideline!*
- Which team is the stickiest? The Toffees!
- Best position if you don't like football? *Right back – in the locker room!*
- My computer caught the 'Bad-Goalie Virus'. *It can't save a thing.*
- Why did the football field turn into a triangle? *Someone took its corner!*
- Why did the football captain bring a rope to the field? *He was the skipper!*

- How do football players keep cool? *They stay close to the fans!*
- What do you call a Norwich player in the World Cup's knockout stages? *The ref!*

DISCLAIMER

THE EVENTS AND DIALOGUES IN THIS BOOK ARE BASED ON TRUE INCIDENTS AND REAL INDIVIDUALS. WHILE THE CORE EVENTS, DATES, AND ACHIEVEMENTS ARE FACTUAL, SOME DIALOGUES AND MINOR DETAILS HAVE BEEN FICTIONALIZED FOR NARRATIVE PURPOSES AND TO MAKE THE CONTENT ENGAGING FOR OUR TARGET AGE GROUP. ANY RESEMBLANCE TO PERSONS, LIVING OR DEAD, OR ACTUAL EVENTS IS PURELY COINCIDENTAL AND NOT INTENDED TO CAUSE ANY HARM OR MISREPRESENTATION. ALL RIGHTS TO THE NAMES AND LIKENESSES OF INDIVIDUALS, TEAMS, AND ORGANIZATIONS MENTIONED IN THIS BOOK ARE OWNED BY THEIR RESPECTIVE COPYRIGHT AND TRADEMARK HOLDERS. THIS BOOK IS MEANT FOR ENTERTAINMENT AND EDUCATIONAL PURPOSES AND NOT FOR COMMERCIAL EXPLOITATION OF THE NAMES INVOLVED.